MARITIME COMMERCE SECURITY PLAN

FOR
THE NATIONAL STRATEGY FOR MARITIME SECURITY

OCTOBER 2005

FOREWORD

By signing National Security Presidential Directive 41/Homeland Security Presidential Directive 13 (NSPD-41/HSPD-13) President Bush underscored the importance of securing the Maritime Domain, which is defined as *"All areas and things of, on, under, relating to, adjacent to, or bordering on a sea, ocean, or other navigable waterway, including all maritime-related activities, infrastructure, people, cargo, and vessels and other conveyances."* NSPD-41/HSPD-13 established a Maritime Security Policy Coordinating Committee (MSPCC)—the first coordinating committee specifically tasked to address this issue—to oversee the development of a National Strategy for Maritime Security (NSMS) and eight supporting implementation plans:

- **The National Plan to Achieve Maritime Domain Awareness** lays the foundation for an effective understanding of anything associated with the Maritime Domain and identifying threats as early and as distant from our shores as possible.
- **The Global Maritime Intelligence Integration Plan** uses existing capabilities to integrate all available intelligence regarding potential threats to U.S. interests in the Maritime Domain.
- **The Maritime Operational Threat Response Plan** facilitates coordinated U.S. government response to threats against the United States and its interests in the Maritime Domain by establishing roles and responsibilities, which enable the government to respond quickly and decisively.
- **The International Outreach and Coordination Strategy** provides a framework to coordinate all maritime security initiatives undertaken with foreign governments and international organizations, and solicits international support for enhanced maritime security.
- **Maritime Infrastructure Recovery Plan** recommends procedures and standards for the recovery of the maritime infrastructure following attack or similar disruption.
- **Maritime Transportation System Security Plan** responds to the President's call for recommendations to improve the national and international regulatory framework regarding the maritime domain.
- **Maritime Commerce Security Plan** establishes a comprehensive plan to secure the maritime supply chain.
- **The Domestic Outreach Plan** engages non-Federal input to assist with the development and implementation of maritime security policies resulting from NSPD-41/HSPD-13.

Although these plans address different aspects of maritime security, they are mutually linked and reinforce each other. Together, NSMS and its supporting plans represent the beginning of a comprehensive national effort to promote global economic stability and protect legitimate activities, while preventing hostile or illegal acts within the Maritime Domain.

TABLE OF CONTENTS

I. INTRODUCTION

"A strong world economy enhances our national security by advancing prosperity and freedom in the rest of the world. Economic growth supported by free trade and free markets creates new jobs and higher incomes. It allows people to lift their lives out of poverty, spurs economic and legal reform, and the fight against corruption, and it reinforces the habits of liberty."

National Security Strategy of the United States of America
September, 2002

The Maritime Commerce Security Plan contains recommendations to promote international supply chain security. The Maritime Commerce Security Plan is a component of the National Strategy for Maritime Security. The National Strategy for Maritime Security was produced in response to National Security Presidential Directive NSPD-41/ Homeland Security Presidential Directive HSPD-13 ("Maritime Security Policy" December 21, 2004). This plan also supports the *National Security Strategy,* the *National Strategy for Homeland Security,* and the *National Strategy for Combating Terrorism.*

The Maritime Commerce Security Plan was developed in conjunction with the other component plans of the National Strategy for Maritime Security. In particular, the development of the Maritime Transportation System Security Plan and the Maritime Infrastructure Recovery Plan was closely coordinated with this plan. The Maritime Transportation System Security Plan addresses the security of the maritime transportation system as a system including vessels, facilities and ports that contribute so greatly to cargo security and, in this way, complements this plan.

The Maritime Infrastructure Recovery Plan also supports this plan because it enhances our ability to minimize the economic impact of an attack or other disruption of the maritime transportation system. This includes effective communication so that private sector organizations have the appropriate information to implement their contingency plans quickly.

This is a risk management plan. As such, it is dependent on reliable information and intelligence to evaluate threats and assess risk. For this reason, the National Plan to Achieve Maritime Domain Awareness and the Global Maritime Intelligence Integration Plan are very important to the success of the Maritime Commerce Security Plan.

All of the component plans of the national strategy provide important support for the improvement of supply chain security. None of these plans should be considered as an independent solution, but together they form an integrated strategy.

II. OVERVIEW OF MARITIME COMMERCE SECURITY

BACKGROUND

Maritime security has been important to the United States since its earliest days. The importance of protecting the Maritime Domain was recognized by our Founding Fathers, who identified national defense, protecting the coast, and detecting smuggling as among the first responsibilities of the new federal government. More than two hundred years later, maritime commerce security remains critical to the national security and economic health of the United States.

Containerized cargo has made the maritime transportation process so efficient that transportation costs are no longer a significant barrier to international trade. Low transportation costs combined with free trade agreements have created an explosive growth in global trade, raising our standard of living. This efficient global supply chain now stretches from the far reaches of the planet directly into the heartland of America.

Maritime transportation of bulk, break-bulk and containerized cargo is the primary mechanism, and in many cases, the only feasible one, for moving goods and commodities around the world quickly and cheaply. The ships that ply the Maritime Domain are the primary mode of transportation for world trade, carrying over 80%[1] of world trade by volume, making the security of the Maritime Domain critically important to the prosperity and liberty of billions of people. Improving the security of this complex supply chain is critical for our national security.

THE CHALLENGE

The Maritime Domain is no longer a great barrier isolating or protecting populations. As modern communications and transport bring the world's population closer together, the oceans have become avenues of connectivity rather than barriers of separation. Disruptions can have immediate and significant global economic impact.

No one nation can single-handedly secure the world's oceans and waterways. Given the indispensable role of the oceans in almost every facet of life, it is in the vital interest of every nation – even those without direct access to the Maritime Domain – to see that the Maritime Domain remains secure for the free and legitimate use of all.

The terrorist attacks of September 11, 2001, demonstrated how our own transportation system could be used as a weapon against the United States. We now recognize the vulnerability

---

[1] Organisation for Economic Co-operation and Development, *Security in Maritime Transport: Risk Factors and Economic Impact,* Maritime Transport Committee, July 2003, p. 6 (http://www.oecd.org/dataoecd/63/13/ 4375896.pdf).

presented by the maritime transportation system. Vessels that anchor at the heart of some of our greatest cities could be used as platforms to launch attacks on our population centers.

The vulnerability is not limited to U.S. seaport cities. The maritime transportation system is the backbone of the intermodal supply chain, which is capable of delivering a 40-foot long closed shipping container from any point in the world to any point in the United States. Suddenly the ubiquitous metal containers visible on highways throughout the nation could represent hidden threats.

The maritime transportation system is vulnerable because it could be used as a conduit for terrorists and their weapons. This threat is not limited to containerized cargo. Our traditional approach to foreign cargo security has been to inspect cargo before it enters the commerce of the United States; however, this is after it has already come to rest in our seaport cities. Although this is a reasonable approach for intercepting contraband, it is not an adequate response to the terrorist threat. This response would be too late to deter an attack on a vessel, a port, and our maritime transportation system in general. That is why the United States' security strategy must create opportunities to intercept threats well before they reach the country's borders.

Maritime commerce could be used to transport a wide spectrum of threats. These threats include nuclear, chemical, biological, radiological, and high explosive weapons, weapon components, narcotics, currency, stowaways, and prohibited or restricted commodities. From a risk management perspective, the threat with the greatest consequences would be the use of the maritime transportation system to deliver a nuclear weapon. A nuclear terrorist attack would have a devastating impact. Depending on where the attack occurred, estimates of deaths range as high as a million people and economic damage would run in the hundreds of billions of dollars.[2] Threats involving weapons of mass destruction, particularly the nuclear threat, must be considered the preeminent risk as long as intelligence continues to validate the credibility of these threats.

There is some debate about calculating the economic impact of even a brief closure of a major seaport. Some estimates run into the millions of dollars. Other estimates suggest that the economic cost would be in the billions. Nevertheless, there is agreement that any sustained closure of the United States' major seaports will have a significant and rapidly expanding impact on the economy.[3] Since the United States represents nearly 20% of global maritime trade

---

[2] For further discussion see:
Congressional Research Service Report RS21293, *Terrorist Nuclear Attacks on Seaports: Threat and Response*, January 24, 2005 (http://www.fas.org/irp/crs/RS21293.pdf) and ABT Associates, "The Economic Impact of Nuclear Terrorist Attacks on Freight Transport Systems in an Age of Seaport Vulnerability," executive summary, April 30, 2003 (http://www.abtassociates.com/reports/ES-Economic_Impact_of_Nuclear_Terrorist_Attacks.pdf).

[3] For further discussion on the economic impact see:
Stephen S. Cohen, *Economic Impact of a West Coast Dock Shutdown*, University of California at Berkeley, January 2002 (http://www.portmod.org/news/2002/May%202/Cohen%20Final%20Jan%202002.pdf); Organisation for Economic Co-operation and Development, *Security in Maritime Transport: Risk Factors and Economic Impact*, Maritime Transport Committee, July 2003 (http://www.oecd.org/dataoecd/63/13/4375896.pdf); and Peter V. Hall, "We'd Have to Sink the Ships, Impact Studies and the 2002 West Coast Port Lockout," *Economic Development Quarterly*, Vol. 18, No. 4, November 2004.

activity[4], any disruption in the United States would have repercussions affecting economic growth throughout the world.

The United States' response to a terrorist incident will not be an automatic shutdown of the nation's seaports. Instead, a prudent and measured response will be taken based on an assessment, including available intelligence, of the specific incident. The National Strategy for Maritime Security builds an environment in which the nation is protected and the economic consequences of any attack are minimized.

---

[4] National Chamber Foundation of the U.S. Chamber of Commerce, *Trade and Transportation, A Study of North American Port and Intermodal Systems,* Washington, D.C., March 2003, p.1.

III. The Maritime Commerce Security Plan

The Goal

The goal of the Maritime Commerce Security Plan is to improve the security of the maritime supply chain to lower the risk that it will be used to support terrorism, criminal or other unlawful or hostile acts, reduce the vulnerability of the Maritime Domain, and protect and facilitate lawful maritime commerce. These improvements in the security of the maritime supply chain will be balanced with the need for the free flow of commerce.

This goal will be achieved by creating a framework that will support the identification of threats as early as possible, even before they enter the Maritime Domain. This plan will improve the information available for risk management, invest in technology to identify threats, develop security requirements, and work in partnership with industry and the international community to promote global supply chain security. The plan also contains performance measures that will be used to evaluate success in meeting the goal and the desired end state.

The End State

The desired end state of the Maritime Commerce Security Plan is a fast, safe, efficient, and secure supply chain that transports only authorized persons and cargo.

Scope

The Maritime Commerce Security Plan is focused on the maritime component of international supply chain security. As such, the focus is on maritime cargo. This plan does not cover the security of maritime passenger operations such as cruise ships and passenger ferries. Cargo security is intertwined with the security of the ports and vessels, which are specifically addressed in the Maritime Transportation System Security Plan.

The threat assessment of cargo is not limited in scope to information regarding the cargo alone, but rather must encompass the totality of the transportation process including the vessel(s), crew, ports of call and intermodal connections. The information requirements for the cargo threat assessments are supported by and supportive of the Maritime Domain Awareness Plan.

Maritime cargo can be subdivided into bulk (dry and liquid), break-bulk, roll-on/roll-off and containerized. Bulk cargo represents the largest segment by weight, while containerized cargo represents the largest segment by value.[5] Looking at the supply chain as an end-to-end process,

---

[5] In 2003, containerized cargo represented over 60% of the value of U.S. waterborne import and export cargo, but only 13% of the tonnage. U.S. Maritime Administration, Waterborne Databank (http://www.marad.dot.gov/statistics/usfwts/PR2003/PRDEC2003.htm).

---

there are intermodal connections to the maritime transportation system. Trucks, railroads, and pipelines (and occasionally aircraft) complete the supply chain by moving cargo to and from the Maritime Domain.

The Maritime Commerce Security Plan addresses the full scope of this international supply chain, but the focus remains on the Maritime Domain. The nature of the threat makes inbound international cargo the priority with special attention paid to containerized cargo because of the unique threat presented by millions of steel containers moving potentially unauthorized cargo and stowaways around the world. This attention does not diminish the importance of securing other types of maritime cargo.

This plan does not alter existing authorities or responsibilities of the department and agency heads, including their authorities, to carry out operational activities or to provide or receive information. This plan is intended only to improve the internal management of the Executive Branch and is not intended to, and does not, create any right or benefit enforceable at law or in equity by any party against the United States, its departments, agencies, entities, officers, employees, agents, or any other person.

ROLES AND RESPONSIBILITIES

The nature of the international supply chain requires a global perspective and extensive interagency coordination. Security considerations must include the extensive intermodal connections that support the international and domestic maritime transportation system including highway, railway and pipelines both here and around the world. With such a wide spectrum of activities, there are many federal departments and agencies that play a significant role in maritime commerce security. These include the Department of Commerce, the Department of Defense, the Department of Energy, the Department of Homeland Security, the Department of State, and the Department of Transportation. State and local authorities also play a critical role in ensuring the security of maritime commerce. Close coordination and cooperation among all these parties is critical for success.

The Department of Homeland Security, with the U.S. Coast Guard as its executive agent, has been assigned the lead role in maritime homeland security for the federal government. That lead is further divided within the Department of Homeland Security with the U.S. Coast Guard having the lead for port and vessel security, Customs and Border Protection having the lead for international cargo security, and the Transportation Security Administration having the lead for domestic intermodal security.

The DHS Office of Policy, Planning and International Affairs is responsible for the integration of maritime commerce security initiatives within the Department of Homeland Security. The Science and Technology Directorate is responsible for supporting the Department of Homeland Security maritime commerce security activities through research, development, testing and evaluation. The Domestic Nuclear Detection Office will also have a central role in developing and coordinating nuclear detection capabilities.

Because the international supply chain is primarily owned and operated by the private sector, maritime commerce security is dependent on the individual efforts of shippers, carriers, consolidators, terminal operators, and many other parties involved in the business process. These same parties would bear the majority of the economic consequences of a maritime transportation incident. This role creates a private sector responsibility to reduce the vulnerability of private sector critical assets and to develop operational procedures and technology to improve security. Private sector action to embed security into commercial practices combined with governmental initiatives to balance security and trade facilitation will create the optimal solutions to manage this threat. Industry/government partnerships, federal advisory committees, outreach activities, and international gatherings will continue to provide opportunities to share best practices and maintain effective lines of communication.

STRATEGIC REQUIREMENTS

The Maritime Commerce Security Plan balances security requirements with the need to maintain the flow of international commerce. The strategy must not unreasonably hinder the free flow of goods.

The cost of securing the supply chain should not be so great that the transportation process becomes a barrier to free trade. Security requirements should be flexible enough and contain viable options to maintain maritime transportation security while connecting with emerging markets.

Security technology is evolving. The plan must provide for adjustments as the technology matures, including issues of compatibility, standardization, and integration with information systems. Priority should be given to effective security solutions that complement and improve the business process and build a foundation for 21st century global trade. A more secure supply chain also can be a more efficient supply chain.

Layered security with multiple opportunities to mitigate threats is better than a single point defense. The ability to identify threats earlier in the supply chain is desirable, particularly before the cargo enters the Maritime Domain and is loaded on vessels.

THE FRAMEWORK

In its simplest form, maritime commerce security requires that the cargo is secure when it is loaded, and that it remains secure during transit. The framework to achieve this objective is best described in terms of five parts: (1) accurate data, (2) secure cargo, (3) secure vessels/ports, (4) secure transit, and (5) international standards and compatible regulations.

(1) Accurate data in the form of advance electronic information is necessary to support the risk assessment of the cargo. This assessment identifies cargo that may present a threat and thus may require some type of intervention. This information is needed early in the process to identify high-risk cargo before it enters the Maritime Domain.

(2) Secure cargo requires a procedure to ensure that the cargo to be loaded on the vessel conforms to the cargo information electronically transmitted to the authorities. This process connects first-hand knowledge of the cargo with the validation of the cargo information. This process also ensures that safeguards are in place to prevent unlawful materials (or persons) from being combined with the legitimate cargo. As an example, this process would involve security procedures to prevent unauthorized cargo and stowaways from being added to a container while it is being packed (stuffed) at a factory. This part also includes a risk management process that includes the inspection (physical inspection and/or the use of non-intrusive inspection equipment) of cargo identified as high risk prior to loading at foreign ports and, in some cases, after arrival at the U.S. port.

(3) Secure vessels and ports protect the security of the cargo while it is in the Maritime Domain. The Maritime Commerce Security Plan will not focus on this element of maritime commerce security. The security of vessels and foreign and domestic ports is supported by the security requirements of the Maritime Transportation Security Act, the International Ship and Port Facility Security Code, and other requirements such as the advance notice of arrival regulations. The Maritime Transportation Security Act regulations specifically address the cargo handling security requirements for vessels and maritime facilities (33 CFR 104-105). Improvements to the national and international regulatory framework are covered in the Maritime Transportation System Security Plan.

(4) Secure transit is a procedure designed to ensure that the secure cargo remains in that status as it enters and moves through the Maritime Domain. Successful implementation requires a method of detecting that security has been compromised during transit and a response protocol to determine if the cargo has remained secure.

(5) Improvements to security within the first four parts of the framework must be addressed in a way that will ensure consistency and substantive improvements across the supply chain. An important way to achieve this goal is to engage appropriate international organizations (e.g. the World Customs Organization, the International Maritime Organization, and the International Organization for Standardization) in the development of standards. Standards are the only meaningful way that the government will be able to ensure that a certain level of security across the supply chain can be expected and achieved. Accurate data, secure cargo, and secure transit goals are all areas where internationally accepted standards would substantially improve the system. Secure vessels/ports is one area that is already subject to consistent international standards through the International Ship and Port Facility Security Code and associated domestic regulations.

THE RISK MANAGEMENT APPROACH

A risk management approach to securing the cargo is the most reasonable approach that will meet the objective of balancing security with the desire to maintain the free flow of commerce. The physical examination of all maritime cargo arriving in the United States would quickly bring maritime commerce to a standstill. International and domestic cargo is vulnerable to a wide spectrum of risks. A risk management approach uses information to stratify the cargo into levels of risk. Resources are then directed toward the high-risk cargo.

The traditional role of customs administrations is to inspect cargo to verify that it is compliant with trade regulations. This often requires a very detailed physical inspection by a well-trained customs officer. However, this trade compliance risk does not need to be detected before the cargo is loaded on a vessel destined for the United States. A customs inspection after the cargo has arrived in the United States is appropriate to mitigate this type of risk.

Although trade compliance is important, the focus of the Maritime Commerce Security Plan is on improving the security of the maritime aspect of the international supply chain. Therefore, a risk management approach to meet these unique risks will require a different approach. Maritime security now involves risks that must be met with a layered approach that identifies and interdicts the threat as far as possible from the U.S. borders. A potential worst case scenario is the risk that a weapon of mass destruction is concealed in a container. Such a threat has severe consequences and must be detected as early as possible. A successful strategy will use risk management to align capabilities with threats to achieve the optimal response and protect the nation.

CURRENT INITIATIVES

There have been a number of important initiatives that have created the first layers of maritime commerce security. A summary of these programs is provided here because the Maritime Commerce Security Plan builds upon these resources and knowledge to create a framework for future action.

Advance Electronic Cargo Information

The 24-Hour Rule, implemented by Customs and Border Protection in December 2002, for the first time required advance information for inbound containerized and break-bulk shipments. This requirement for an advance cargo declaration 24 hours before the cargo is laden aboard the vessel at a foreign port represented a significant change in the flow of information, allowing the United States to identify threats earlier in the maritime transportation process. However, under the 24-Hour Rule, the information could be submitted as paper documentation that required a manual review of thousands of pages of cargo declarations. In addition, bulk shipments were exempt. The Trade Act of 2002 (PL 107-210), as amended by the Maritime Transportation Security Act of 2002, rectified this problem by requiring the electronic transmission of cargo information (inbound and outbound) for all modes of transportation (vessel, air, rail, and truck).

The Automated Targeting System

The Automated Targeting System used by Customs and Border Protection is a rules-based analytical tool that uses cargo information, law enforcement information, and historical data, along with information from the intelligence community, to assess the risk posed by the cargo. The availability of cargo information much earlier in the process created an environment in which the risk assessment of cargo takes place even before the cargo was loaded on vessels at foreign ports. This system supports the assessment of all types of maritime cargo and is not limited to containerized cargo.

Non-Intrusive Inspection Equipment

Today, large scale gamma-ray imaging systems can scan entire containers in minutes, creating a high resolution image of their contents. Some of these systems are capable of imaging the contents of rail cars as moving trains pass by the system. Other types of equipment currently in use to inspect international cargo have the ability to detect nuclear and radiological threats. Radiation Portal Monitors identify radiation sources in moving vehicles as they pass by the detectors. Radiation Isotope Identifier devices are handheld instruments that further identify the source of radiation. Personal Radiation Detectors are pager-sized devices that are used to detect and localize sources of radiation.

The increasing availability and effectiveness of non-intrusive inspection equipment supports the objective of improving security while maintaining the flow of international commerce. There are limitations to this technology, but as detection technology improves, the labor-intensive physical inspection of cargo for security threats will become less necessary.

Container Security Initiative

The Container Security Initiative began in 2002 and has quickly expanded to major foreign seaports from which the majority of container shipments to the United States originate. Through bilateral agreements, Customs and Border Protection officers are stationed at foreign seaports where they work with the host government to identify high-risk shipments before they are shipped to the United States. Customs and Border Protection and Immigration and Customs Enforcement officers work together with their host government counterparts to target and pre-screen containers and to develop additional investigative leads related to the terrorist threat to cargo destined for the United States.

This innovative program became possible because of the availability of advance electronic cargo information, automated tools such as the Automated Targeting System to use that information, non-intrusive inspection technology to efficiently inspect high-risk containers, and an international community committed to the improvement of maritime security. The Container Security Initiative is a program that supports the objective of identifying high-risk cargo earlier in the supply chain, ideally before the cargo enters the Maritime Domain.

Megaports Initiative

The Department of Energy's National Nuclear Security Administration is actively pursuing international cooperation to equip 24 key seaports with passive radiation detection equipment to screen containerized cargo. The Megaports Initiative will also provide training to appropriate law enforcement officials to provide them with the technical means to deter, detect, and interdict illicit trafficking in nuclear and other radioactive materials. This expertise is based on years of experience equipping international seaports, airports and vehicle crossings with radiation detection and related communications equipment and response systems. The specialized radiation detection technology was developed by Department of Energy laboratories as part of the overall U.S. nuclear security program to guard against proliferation of weapons materials.

Customs-Trade Partnership against Terrorism

The Customs-Trade Partnership against Terrorism (C-TPAT) is an industry and government partnership to improve overall supply chain security. In C-TPAT, Customs and Border Protection has partnered with the trade community to implement security criteria and best practices that better protect the entire supply chain against exploitation by terrorists.

C-TPAT uses the leverage that major importers have over their suppliers to improve security. C-TPAT importers go as far as mandating security procedures in their contracts with foreign suppliers, specifying the security procedures that must be observed before products are loaded and shipped to the United States. The C-TPAT program has a validation procedure in which Customs and Border Protection officers verify that the C-TPAT members have actually implemented the security procedures they have outlined to the government. In exchange for improving the security of the supply chain, these companies are qualified to receive expedited clearance of their cargo.

Operation Safe Commerce

Operation Safe Commerce is the federal government's pilot project to evaluate the effectiveness of various technologies and business practices in ensuring international supply chain and container security from foreign point of origin to its U.S. destination. Operation Safe Commerce has examined the security of a variety of supply chains to identify vulnerabilities and measure the effectiveness of operational best practices and different types of technology to address those vulnerabilities. Operation Safe Commerce has allowed us to understand better the complexity of supply chain security from origin to destination, the impact of security technologies and business practices on supply chains, and the limits of current technology.

INTERNATIONAL COOPERATION

We have seen unprecedented international cooperation in raising the level of maritime transportation security. The Container Security Initiative and the Megaports Initiative are just two of many international efforts. Another excellent example is the International Ship and Port Facility Security Code adopted by the International Maritime Organization on December 12, 2002. This code is a set of comprehensive measures to enhance the security of ships and port facilities. It provides a consistent framework for vessel and port risk assessments.

Another important effort is the Proliferation Security Initiative (PSI). The PSI is a global effort that aims to stop the proliferation of weapons of mass destruction, their delivery systems and related material to and from states and non-state actors of proliferation concern by developing partnerships and cooperating in interdiction and interdiction exercises. PSI participants are committed to acting consistently with national legal authorities and relevant international law and frameworks. The United States has signed bilateral ship-boarding agreements with three major flag states (Panama, Liberia, and the Marshall Islands) and is pursuing similar agreements with more than 20 others; these agreements are tangible examples of nonproliferation cooperation and establish expedited processes to board vessels suspected of carrying weapons of mass destruction related shipments. This effort shows the clear commitment of the international community that the global transportation system will not be used to support weapons of mass destruction proliferation.

The United States continues to actively promote the proposed amendments to the Convention for the Suppression of Unlawful Acts Against the Safety of Maritime Navigation (SUA Convention), which seeks to criminalize the illicit transport by commercial ships in international waters of weapons of mass destruction, their delivery systems, and related materials and the recently adopted International Convention for the Suppression of Acts of Nuclear Terrorism, which obligates States to criminalize the possession, use and release of certain radioactive materials or devices with the intent to cause or threaten death, serious bodily injury or substantial damage to property or the environment. These agreements directly support other U.S. efforts to address maritime security issues, such as the Proliferation Security Initiative and other U.S. government policy initiatives and programs.

The Department of Homeland Security has been working with the international community to ensure we are addressing cargo security from a global perspective. Customs and Border Protection is currently working with members of the World Customs Organization to address global supply chain security. This includes standards for Customs-to-Customs and Customs-to-Business relationships. Four areas of discussion are: (1) the harmonization of advance electronic manifest requirements on inbound, outbound and transit shipments; (2) a standardized risk management approach; (3) inspection of outbound cargo at the request of the destination country using non-intrusive detection equipment, such as large scale X-ray machines and radiation detectors; and (4) concrete benefits to businesses that meet minimal supply chain security standards and best practices.

The Export Control and Related Border Security Assistance Program, funded and coordinated by the Department of State, with support from the Department of Defense, Department of Commerce, and Department of Homeland Security/Customs and Border Protection, assists 45 other countries in strengthening export controls to prevent weapons of mass destruction, their delivery systems, and related materials from entering the supply chain. The program enhances the ability of foreign customs and border security agencies to screen cargo to detect, interdict, and prosecute the illicit transport such items by providing equipment at ports of entry/exit including x-ray, portal monitoring, and other weapons of mass destruction detection capabilities, as well as the requisite training to identify suspect materials.

These are but a few of the important international efforts that directly or indirectly support maritime commerce security. As we move forward in securing the Maritime Domain, our ability to work in partnership with other shipping and trading nations and, together with them, to articulate a thoughtful and effective strategy, will continue to elicit the support of the international community.

IV. THE WAY FORWARD

The four foundations of the *National Strategy for Homeland Security* are Law, Science and Technology, Information Sharing and Systems, and International Cooperation. The Maritime Commerce Security Plan shares these foundations. The way forward requires a long term perspective that will require new regulations, improved technology, additional sources of information, and extensive international cooperation. The plan recommendations reflect these four foundations.

The core of maritime commerce is composed of major carriers operating out of major seaports. As we push back to feeder vessels, smaller ports, intermodal connections and hundreds of thousands of shippers and producers around the world, our knowledge about the parties involved becomes more and more limited. The flow of commercial information travels its own separate route, eventually linking buyer and seller. This end-to-end flow of information must be tapped to support the risk assessment of cargo.

Tracking the flow of cargo from where the product is produced or packaged to its final point of delivery is appealing as a security solution. This end-to-end approach provides potential business benefits for loss prevention, inventory control, and in-transit visibility. However, this is not the only road to maritime security. Our framework requires that cargo entering the Maritime Domain be secure. This can be achieved by securing cargo long before it enters the Maritime Domain and then tracking it from that point until it is loaded on the vessel. Securing the cargo before it enters the Maritime Domain can also be achieved by a certified third party validating the security of the cargo before it is loaded on the vessel.

Rather than mandating a solution requiring levels of technology that some economies cannot support, this plan supports multiple solutions to keep an open global marketplace. There are clear benefits to end-to-end physical controls, but protecting cargo from loss, theft, or damage before it reaches the Maritime Domain is not a priority for maritime commerce security.

As supply chain technology matures and information systems develop, there will be new options for ensuring the security of maritime commerce, particularly when a stronger business case can be made for the use of this technology. The Support Anti-Terrorism by Fostering Effective Technologies or SAFETY Act provides limited liability protection to companies and manufacturers so that they are not deterred from developing security solutions. This Act may be helpful in bringing creative private sector ingenuity to the challenge of international supply chain security. There also will be opportunities for international cooperation in building capacity throughout the world to support more advanced information systems and the overall risk management approach to cargo processing.

We are now looking for threats that should never enter the Maritime Domain. This will require new levels of international cooperation to support programs like the Container Security Initiative so that risk assessments and non-intrusive inspection technology can be used before cargo leaves the international harbors. The catastrophic threat of weapons of mass destruction creates a need to have comprehensive nuclear and radiological detection capabilities at the world's ports.

Another part of maritime security involves keeping the cargo secure during transit. This too is variable. If cargo is secured at an inland point, it must remain secure during the entire journey forward. If the security is compromised before it reaches the Maritime Domain, it must be secured again before it can be loaded. Once the secure cargo enters the Maritime Domain, it must be secure to its destination port. How this is achieved will depend on the cargo. The vessel itself is the container for bulk cargo – procedures to secure the vessel also secure bulk cargo. Containerized cargo, on the other hand, will require its own unique security procedures to provide security to both the container and the vessel that is carrying it.

RECOMMENDATIONS

In order to create a comprehensive approach to improve maritime commerce security, and achieve the desired end state, this plan builds upon and enhances current efforts to achieve greater levels of security. The plan recommendations are divided into five categories reflecting the five parts of the strategic framework. They represent the broad government approach necessary to defend the international supply chain against the terrorist threat.

Accurate Data

The risk management approach is dependent on timely and accurate information. The 24-Hour Rule was a significant breakthrough that created a revolution in our approach to maritime commerce security. The Trade Act of 2002, as amended by the Maritime Transportation Security Act of 2002, has promulgated this approach by requiring advance electronic cargo information for all modes of transportation. That law also recognized the importance of reliable information providing guidance that data should come from those most likely to have direct knowledge of that information.

The objective is to obtain the critical information necessary to assess reliably the risk of individual cargo transactions. There are many parties with pieces of information that taken together can form a complete picture. The buyers, sellers, shippers and carriers form the outline, but the information process is dynamic. Goods are resold while on the move. The risk assessment must be equally dynamic, acquiring information from multiple sources to capture an end-to-end data perspective on each transaction.

Recommendation: The Department of Homeland Security, in consultation with the trade community, will develop a plan to obtain additional advance electronic information to support cargo risk assessments. This should include an evaluation of current data used for the customs release of commercial cargo (entry level data) to determine its value for risk assessment and the availability of this data prior to the lading of vessels at foreign ports.

Recommendation: The international supply chain is complex and lengthy. The risk assessment of cargo should consider the widest possible view of the supply chain. This includes vessel and port information. The Department of Homeland Security will ensure that the U.S. Coast Guard's foreign port assessment information and vessel security plan compliance histories will be available to Customs and Border Protection for use in cargo targeting and selectivity activities. The U.S. Coast Guard will work with Customs and Border Protection to supply this information in a form that will best support and enhance the Automated Targeting System.

Recommendation: Customs and Border Protection has begun a new project called the Advanced Trade Data Initiative that builds upon existing security measures to gather and analyze specific information already existing in commercial supply chain participants' databases. The Advanced Trade Data Initiative will allow greater visibility deeper into and throughout the supply chain for more informed decision-making. Customs and Border Protection will continue pursuing additional information through this initiative and improve Maritime Domain awareness.

Recommendation: The Department of Homeland Security will continue the rapid development of the enhanced capabilities of the Automated Commercial Environment to support the Automated Targeting System and improve the risk analysis and targeting capabilities.

Recommendation: The Maritime Domain Awareness Plan will bring greater transparency to threats within the Maritime Domain. Maritime Domain Awareness should support and be supported by the cargo assessment process. The Departments of Homeland Security, Defense, and Transportation will work together to integrate the cargo risk assessment process and efforts to enhance Maritime Domain awareness.

Secure Cargo

This is the most difficult part of the maritime security framework. It consists of the development of business security procedures to secure containerized cargo at the point of stuffing (loaded into an intermodal container) and that other types of cargo are secure before they are loaded on vessels. Since this activity takes place outside the United States, there is limited regulatory authority to require specific security practices. The Customs-Trade Partnership against Terrorism has developed security criteria that participants must follow when loading containers to prevent illegitimate materials from being inserted during this phase of the supply chain. Expanding industry and government partnerships, combined with international cooperation, will be necessary to embed the essential security procedures into common business practices.

The second part of secure cargo is the use of risk management and non-intrusive inspection equipment to verify that the cargo really is secure. The Maritime Commerce Security Plan has a priority objective of expanding the capacity to screen for weapons of mass destruction. The consequences of a nuclear attack through maritime cargo are so great that it must be the first priority. The world's seaports must become a barrier to nuclear proliferation. The longer term objective is to develop a large scale capability to detect rapidly the full spectrum of weapons of mass destruction or effect which include chemical, biological, radiological, nuclear, and high explosive threats.

Recommendation: The Department of Homeland Security in consultation with the Departments of State, Commerce, and Transportation will develop and recommend standards for the loading (stuffing) of containers before the cargo reaches the Maritime Domain, and procedures for securing other types of cargo before loading on a vessel destined to or from the United States. These procedures should include, but not be limited to, security recommendations for bulk, break-bulk, and vehicles transported on auto carrier vessels.

Recommendation: As part of the effort to develop recommended standards, the Department of Homeland Security will work with the World Customs Organization to develop internationally recognized cargo security standards for the secure "stuffing" of containers in international trade. This will include procedures to ensure that prohibited and dangerous materials are not placed in the container when it is being loaded.

Recommendation: The Department of Homeland Security will develop a plan to deploy radiation portal monitors or more advanced technology at all domestic seaports that receive international cargo, with the objective of screening every vehicle and rail car entering and leaving the facility for radiation. This will create a domestic layer of defense while demonstrating to foreign ports that detection technology can be integrated into a port operation without adversely affecting operations.

Recommendation: The Department of Homeland Security will work with the Department of Energy and the Department of State to develop a plan under the Megaports Initiative to equip foreign ports with sensor technology to detect nuclear and radioactive materials, creating an opportunity to detect weapons of mass destruction at both domestic and foreign ports.

Recommendation: The Department of Homeland Security will support maritime security by coordinating efforts in detecting nuclear/radiological material with the Department of Energy. This will include the development of enhanced Radiation Portal Monitors and the development of similar equipment to detect nuclear/radiological threats in other types of maritime cargo including liquid and dry bulk cargo.

Recommendation: The Department of Homeland Security, in cooperation with other federal agencies, will support maritime commerce security through the development of reliable non-intrusive detection technology for chemical/biological/explosives threats in maritime cargo.

Secure Vessels/Ports

The Maritime Transportation System Security Plan addresses the security of vessels, facilities and ports. These security procedures are important since the protection of the vessel, facility and port also serves to protect the cargo. Security procedures must be in place to prevent the smuggling on board of weapons of mass destruction/effect and other dangerous materials while the vessel is in port or in transit. These procedures should also prevent illegal migration (stowaways).

Recommendation: The Department of Homeland Security will regularly review the Maritime Transportation Security Act regulations regarding security requirements and cargo controls for ports and vessels to identify any areas needing changes as cargo control procedures evolve.

Recommendation: The Federal Maritime Security Coordinators should encourage cargo owners (if not already engaged) to participate on Area Maritime Security Committees to bring their perspective and expertise to the Committees.

Recommendation: The Department of Homeland Security and the Departments of Commerce, State, and Transportation will consider ways to improve communication with cargo owners as they develop overall communication plans for responding to a maritime transportation security incident.

Secure Transit

The next stage of a secure system is a method to verify that the initially secure cargo remains secure throughout the journey. For many types of cargo, such as liquid or dry bulk, the vessel itself is the cargo container. In these cases, we rely on the security procedures for the vessel to secure the cargo during transit.

Containerized cargo presents a different situation. The *National Strategy for Homeland Security* specifically created a mandate to "increase the security of international shipping containers." In some ways, containerized cargo has two layers of protection since it is protected by the container and by the vessel during the voyage. However, it also is more dangerous because the container may have a very long unprotected journey before it is loaded on the vessel. Supply chain studies have identified the many vulnerabilities of containerized cargo as it makes it way from the inland point where it was loaded until it reaches the harbor. A secure system must be able to detect whether or not the security of the container has been compromised before it is allowed to enter the Maritime Domain.

The cost of technologies to monitor goods in transit, such as radio frequency identification (RFID) technology, is reaching a price point that may create a business case for more widespread use. The Department of Defense is already a major user of radio frequency identification technology for military logistics. As the market evolves, there may be opportunities to tap such technologies and integrate them into information systems that could support maritime commerce security. It is important for the U.S. government to continue reviewing technological innovations and enhanced operational procedures that may be useful for supply chain security.

Several federal departments and agencies are currently engaged in initiatives to enhance and improve the security of containerized cargo supply chains. The Department of Homeland Security Science and Technology Directorate has embarked on a number of container technology initiatives, including the development of an Advanced Container Security Device, along with research on RFID technology and container security system communications. These initiatives will keep the Department of Homeland Security well informed on emerging technology and add to the knowledge already gained from Operation Safe Commerce.

Industry/government partnerships (like the Customs-Trade Partnership against Terrorism) will continue to be a valuable source of information on industry best practices and real world solutions to supply chain security. Of course, Federal Advisory Committees and industry outreach will also inform future decisions on voluntary guidelines and regulatory requirements for technological solutions to maritime security. International cooperation on procedures and agreements on standards will also pave the way for future security improvements.

Recommendation: As an immediate step to increasing the security of international shipping containers, the Department of Homeland Security will issue an advance notice of proposed rule making requiring that loaded containers being transported to the United States must be secured with an ISO-compliant high security mechanical seal at the last point where the container is loaded (i.e. the last point of stuffing) and before entering the Maritime Domain. The Department of Homeland Security will develop a response protocol for those cases in which a container destined to the United States arrives at the foreign port of lading with a missing or compromised seal.

Recommendation: The Department of Homeland Security will develop and recommend security guidelines for the domestic movement of import and export containerized cargo that are complementary to any seal regulations issued by the Department. This will include an evaluation of the potential impact of implementing comparable regulations for domestic transportation. In addition, current domestic supply chain security procedures for cargo shipped from the United States will be evaluated against our security expectations for foreign cargo exported to the United States. We should not have lower standards than we expect from our trading partners.

Recommendation: The Department of Homeland Security will work with the World Customs Organization to develop recommended procedures and/or standards for instances in which high security seals are removed by customs administrations in the course of official export inspections prior to lading.

Recommendation: The Department of Homeland Security will continue research, development, testing and evaluation of technology to secure containerized cargo. This includes the development of the future container, the advanced container security device, and the integration of sensor technology with information systems. This effort will be coordinated with the Department of Defense and other federal departments and agencies involved in similar programs. Information on the effectiveness and practicality of this technology will be used to inform future policy decisions on the security requirements for containerized cargo.

Recommendation: The Department of Homeland Security and the Departments of Commerce, State, and Transportation, will review non-containerized maritime cargo, including bulk, break-bulk, car carriers, and roll-on/roll-off operations, to determine whether additional procedures are needed to improve their security during transit. An action plan will be developed to close any security gaps identified by the review. The action plan will address whether security gaps can be addressed through international standards developed through appropriate international organizations.

Recommendation: The Department of Homeland Security will continue to work with industry through partnership programs like the Customs-Trade Partnership against Terrorism to identify best practices, share information, and gain from the experience of the private sector in applying technology to improve supply chain security and efficiency.

Recommendation: The Department of Homeland Security and the Departments of Commerce and Transportation will identify short and long term actions to improve the security of the domestic intermodal supply chain that connects the nation to the Maritime Domain. This will include a review of any supply chain vulnerabilities that arise at the interface between the maritime transportation system and the domestic intermodal transportation system.

Recommendation: Many of the current Department of Homeland Security initiatives supporting maritime commerce security have been in existence a number of years. In order to confirm that they are fully integrated with the overall national strategy, the Department of Homeland Security will review these programs to ensure that they are properly aligned with the National Strategy for Maritime Security and make any necessary improvements.

International Standards and Regulations

Given the limitations of governmental jurisdiction and direct business influence on the international supply chain, we must use international organizations to develop minimum acceptable standards for security in international trade. This approach has already been successfully implemented, as exemplified by the vessel and facility security standards established by the International Ship and Port Facility Security Code. International standards play a crucial role in reaching foreign portions of the international supply chain that are not influenced by the requirements of any one nation.

Recommendation: The Department of Homeland Security, in coordination with the Departments of State and Transportation, will promote the use of international standards throughout the international supply chain, particularly in the areas of business practices and data management.

Recommendation: The widespread acceptance of the requirement for advance electronic data to support risk management would improve maritime commerce security throughout the world. The Department of Homeland Security will continue its work with the World Customs Organization to promote the international acceptance of this approach.

PERFORMANCE MEASURES

Although plan success could be measured by the absence of a terrorist attack, effectively measuring success in achieving the goals of this plan is complex. There is no simple measure of the security improvements that will result from the Maritime Commerce Security Plan. Instead, progress may be gauged by a blend of measures reflecting different activities.

The characteristics of secure maritime commerce include (1) the ability to provide the government with accurate electronic data to support risk management; (2) procedures to secure cargo before it enters the Maritime Domain; (3) the use of secure vessels and ports; (4) procedures to detect breaches of security during transit; and (5) the development of international standards to address the global nature of the international supply chain.

Success in providing accurate data can be measured by data transmissions that are timely and complete. In addition, random compliance sampling by Customs and Border Protection of imported cargo will verify that the transmitted data conforms to actual cargo shipped.

Customs and Border Protection performs validations of the foreign security procedures of Customs-Trade Partnership against Terrorism participants. This could act as a measure of effectiveness in implementing procedures to secure cargo.

The Maritime Transportation Security Act/International Ship and Port Facility Security Code compliance assessments for vessels and facilities maintained by the U.S. Coast Guard may be used as a measure of the implementation of security measures.

Once a seal regulation is implemented, the frequency of containers arriving at the port of lading with missing or compromised seals can be measured. In the future, more advanced sensors could provide more detailed information on security problems.

Progress in deploying radiation detection technology, measures of the effectiveness of the technology in detecting weapons, along with equipment utilization rates would be indicators of success in implementing this technology.

Additional international agreements on security standards, following the model of the International Ship and Port Facility Security Code, will be another measure of the success of this plan.

Local, national, and international maritime security exercises have the potential to measure improvements in security and also identify security gaps (lessons learned) that require additional action. Similarly, red-teaming (attempting to find vulnerabilities in your own security procedures) can be used to probe maritime commerce security to measure the effectiveness of implemented security procedures.

The intelligence community may detect changes in the strategy of terrorist groups and rogue states caused by perceptions of better security in the Maritime Domain.

The business community may see evidence of better security through lower rates of cargo theft, but this may not be evident immediately because of the uneven reporting of pilferage.

These are a few of the performance measures for maritime commerce security. More detailed measures are being developed for a number of program initiatives. The Department of Homeland Security and other federal agencies will continue working with other departments and agencies and the private sector to further refine performance measures.

V. Conclusion

"We will be resolute. Others might flag in the face of the inevitable ebb and flow against terrorism. But the American people will not. We understand that we cannot choose to disengage from the world, because in this globalized era, the world will engage us regardless. The choice is really about the type of world we want to live in."

National Strategy for Combating Terrorism
February 2003

There are many obstacles in the path to ensuring the security of maritime commerce. The ability of terrorists and criminals to use any type of vulnerability to their advantage, combined with the need to keep international commerce flowing, make commerce security a difficult task. The sheer magnitude of the global supply chain constrains our ability as a nation to prescribe and enforce security standards across its full breadth. The technologies to secure cargo during transit and detect threats hidden within cargo are still evolving. In spite of these challenges, significant progress has already been made. Still, there is much more to be done.

We all share a common interest in keeping destructive forces out of the supply chain. Through partnerships and international cooperation, the global supply chain will become secure and transparent. The more we can integrate security into common business practices and modern information systems, the better we will be able to sustain increased levels of security.

The security of the Maritime Domain is improved by securing the cargo that flows through it. Cargo security mitigates one potential threat to the transportation system. The component plans of the National Strategy for Maritime Security form a whole that is greater than the parts. They build a resilience that will protect maritime commerce and minimize the impact of any attacks. Implementation of this plan will advance United States' national security objectives to prevent terrorist attacks, reduce the vulnerability of the Maritime Domain, and protect lawful maritime commerce